WHY DO I GROW?

BY MADELINE TYLER

BookLife
PUBLISHING

©2018
BookLife Publishing
King's Lynn
Norfolk PE30 4LS

A catalogue record for
this book is available from
the British Library.

ISBN: 978-1-78637-366-3

Written by:
Madeline Tyler

Edited by:
Kirsty Holmes

Designed by:
Danielle Rippengill

Image Credits

All images are courtesy of Shutterstock.com, unless otherwise specified. With thanks to Getty Images, Thinkstock Photo and iStockphoto. Front Cover & 1 – Dmitry Natashin, Nadzin, nasidastudio, grmarc. Images used on every spread – Nadzin, TheFarAwayKingdom. 2 – Roi and Roi. 4–7 – Iconic Bestiary. 8 – eranicle. 9 – MSSA. 10 & 11 – arborelza. 12 & 13 – Iconic Bestiary. 14 – lukpedclub. 15 – Iconic Bestiary, KIKUCHI, ByEmo, Roman Marvel. 16 – Iconic Bestiary. 17 – Ira Yapanda. 18 – Roi and Roi. 19 – LynxVector. 20 – Iconic Bestiary. 21 – svtdesign. 22 – Iconic Bestiary. 23 – user friendly, Anna Violet.

CONTENTS

Words that look like **this** can be found in the glossary on page 24.

How Tall Are You?

Are you tall, short, or somewhere in between?

Do your fingernails always need a **trim**? Or maybe they feel like they are not growing at all?

Has a doctor ever measured how tall you are?

150
140
130
120
110
100
90
80
70
60
50
40
30
20
10

Children grow more and more every day – your bones get bigger and your bodies get taller. Some people grow quickly, and some slowly.

Even adults grow - their hair grows longer and so do their nails.

Growing Up

When we get older, we grow bigger and stronger.

Growing is an important part of getting older and growing up. Even though you are small now, one day you might be even taller than your teacher!

People usually stop growing taller when they are around 18 to 21 years old. However, your hair and nails carry on growing longer until you are very old.

The endocrine system

The endocrine system is made up of things called **glands** and **hormones**.

Glands release hormones into our blood. Hormones carry information and instructions to different **cells** in our body.

There are lots of glands all over your body. They release different hormones that do different jobs. Sometimes, hormone levels can be too high or too low.

Some people inject themselves with hormones if their levels are too low.

9

Glands and Growth

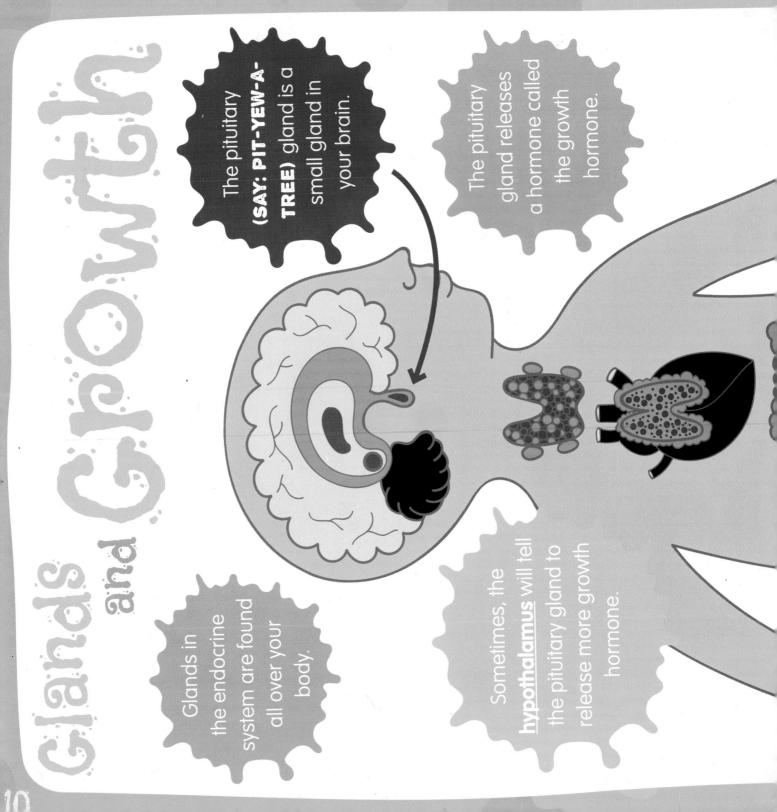

The pituitary (SAY: **PIT-YEW-A-TREE**) gland is a small gland in your brain.

The pituitary gland releases a hormone called the growth hormone.

Glands in the endocrine system are found all over your body.

Sometimes, the **hypothalamus** will tell the pituitary gland to release more growth hormone.

Some other children do not have enough growth hormone. These children do not grow very tall, and their baby teeth do not fall out for a long time.

Grow Your Own Child

Having the right amount of growth hormone is important, but so are lots of other things. To grow a strong and healthy child, you will need:

- Water
- **Calcium**
- Sleep
- Exercise
- Vitamins
- Minerals

Growing is hard work, and very tiring. It is important to look after your body as it is growing, by:

Vitamins and minerals are nutrients that your body gets from food to stay healthy.

Getting the right amount of sleep - not too much and not too little!

Eating healthy food

Exercising

Drinking lots of water

Growth Spurts!

When children are around 11 or 12 years old, they grow very quickly. This is called a growth spurt.

A hormone called testosterone starts the growth spurt.

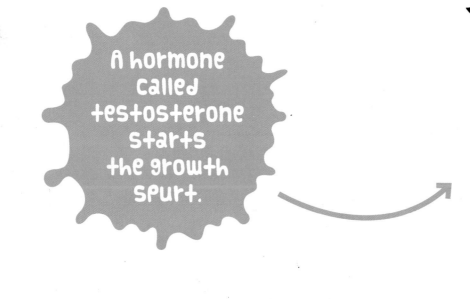

140
130
120
110

20

10

During a growth spurt, the hands and feet grow first. Teenagers often need lots of new shoes because they grow out of them so quickly!

Gross Growth

Toenails

Toenails grow all the time, and not just during a growth spurt. Make sure you trim them regularly so that they do not look like this!

Each toenail grows 19.2 millimetres every year!

Nose Hair

Everybody has nose hair, even little babies. As you get older, your hormone levels change. This makes you grow bushier eyebrows and more ear and nose hair!

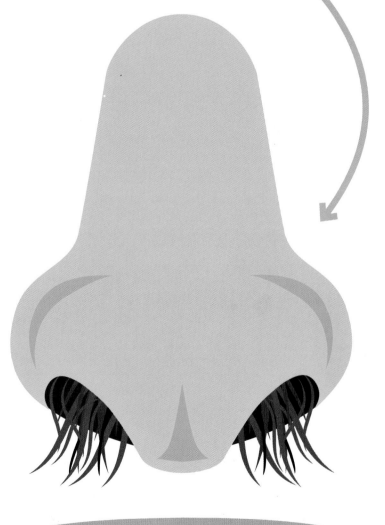

Helpful Hormones

Hormones like the growth hormone help all the parts of your body to grow. Other hormones have different jobs that help your body in other ways.

Sleep

Happiness

Hungry

Energy

Angry

Growth

Insulin controls the levels of sugar in your blood.

Adrenaline makes your heart beat faster. It prepares your body for when you are about to do something scary.

Record Breakers

The shortest person ever to have lived was Chandra Bahadur Dangi. He was 54.6 centimetres (cm) tall!

Robert Wadlow is the tallest man ever to have lived. He was 2.72 m tall - almost a whole metre taller than his dad!

A man called Mehmet Ozyurek has the longest nose on a human. His nose is 8.8 cm long!

The longest ever fingernails were 8.65 metres (m) long!

Glossary

calcium	natural substance used by the body to grow healthy bones and teeth
cells	the basic units that make up all living things
gigantism	a medical condition that leads to people being unusually tall
glands	organs in the body that produce hormones and chemicals
hormones	a chemical in the body that tells cells what to do
hypothalamus	a part of the brain that produces hormones
nutrients	natural substances that plants and animals need to grow and stay healthy
trim	to cut a little bit off something

Index